The Jen-uine Dry Cut™
How To Be A Cut Above The Rest

Jennifer Brumm Lancia

BookLocker
Trenton, Georgia

Copyright © 2024 Jennifer Brumm Lancia

Print ISBN: 978-1-958892-07-7
Ebook ISBN: 979-8-88531-680-4

All rights reserved. No part of this publication may be reproduced, stored in a retrieval system, or transmitted in any form or by any means, electronic, mechanical, recording or otherwise, without the prior written permission of the author.

Published by BookLocker.com, Inc., Trenton, Georgia.

BookLocker.com, Inc.
2024

First Edition

Library of Congress Cataloging in Publication Data
Lancia, Jennifer Brumm
The Jen-uine Dry Cut™ How To Be A Cut Above The Rest by Jennifer Brumm Lancia
Library of Congress Control Number: 2024918443

Table of Contents

Introduction: Why I Wrote This Book 1
Introducing Myself to You 3
Opening My Salon: "The Artistic Edge" 10
And Who Are YOU? 12
Wet Cutting vs. Dry Cutting: The Major Differences 16
So What, Exactly, is a Dry Cut? 18
Twelve Reasons Why Dry is Better 20
Why Does Dry Cutting Take Longer? 27
Help your clients understand why they'll pay more
    for dry cutting 30
How is Dry Cutting Beneficial to Those with
    Extensions or Color? 34
Why Don't More Hairdressers Dry Cut? 36

Introducing: The JEN-UINE DRY CUT™! 38
The Jen-uine Dry Cut™: Is it for you? 38
What is The Jen-uine Dry Cut™? 42

25 Essential Elements of The Jen-uine Dry Cut™ 45
Setting you up to be successful behind the chair -
    every time! 45
The many benefits of The Jen-uine Dry Cut™ 60
Celebrate Your Artistry 68
Finishing: The Cut's Final Stages – and Beyond 72

Conclusion 79

Introduction:
Why I Wrote This Book

THE JEN-UINE DRY CUT™ (*"How To Be A Cut Above The Rest"*) is a manual designed to share my knowledge and experience with both professionals and students in the hair industry. Unlike other instruction books, this one does not focus on diagrams, charts, and labels. Rather, I share my insight on the methods which have worked so well for the past 22 years, where my main focus always has been 100% client satisfaction.

This book spotlights the art of dry cutting, the differences between cutting wet vs. dry, and all of the benefits of dry cutting. You will learn why a dry cut costs more, why it takes longer than a traditional cut, and why I believe every stylist should at least give it a try. I discuss the components I believe are vital to each appointment, such as: working with one client at a time, creating a calm environment, beginning with a thorough consultation, and using intuition while creating.

My goal is to inspire you to work with passion, and to be open to trying new methods. Since hair styling is an art, there really is no "right" or "wrong". I encourage you to embrace your unique talents, and to be the very best version of yourself. My aim is to help you achieve that by introducing new techniques, such as dry cutting, and specifically, **THE JEN-UINE DRY CUT**™.

THE JEN-UINE DRY CUT™ is my version of dry cutting, the technique invented by John Sahag. It is my unique approach to working with each client from before the first appointment through what I hope will be a long-lasting relationship.

I also hope that my outside-the-box approach will inspire you, and help you to realize that you do not have to work exactly how we were taught in school. I encourage you to focus more on customer satisfaction and client retention, rather than getting in as many clients in one day as possible. Working more slowly, or differently from others, is perfectly okay.

As you are no doubt aware, the hair world can be a jealous and competitive industry. That has always saddened me. We are all artists, and all unique in our own ways. I want to encourage you to focus on your own passion, while leaving the drama behind. When we give ourselves complete artistic freedom, including setting the tone of the environment in which we work, we will do our best. We become fueled with passion, and the possibilities are endless!

Introducing Myself to You

Hello there! My name is Jennifer Brumm Lancia. Born in Denville, New Jersey in 1978, I was raised in the middle-class suburbs of Massachusetts, along with my younger brother Michael. Growing up, I was a very friendly little girl. I wanted to include everyone; I just wished everyone would be nice to others.

I was in Girl Scouts, and I played soccer and tennis. Although I did well in many subjects, I thrived in my art classes. From the time I was very young, art was my escape and my passion.

My creative talent for hair emerged early in my life. I loved styling my dolls' hair, and did so whenever given the opportunity. Barbie®, My Little Pony®, and Cabbage Patch Kids™ – I collected any toy with hair, just so I had a chance to style and cut their hair. I always figured out a way to enhance and play with their styles.

While watching television, I would continually study the hair and think to myself what I would want to do differently. I noticed peoples' hair color; I would ponder whether their hair color was the appropriate shade for their skin tone. I would also study the cut. Sometimes, I would think, "a shorter length would look good on her" or "those bangs seem too heavy". I would take note of what I'd change based on that actor's face shape and features. It was apparent to me that some looked more appealing than others in different hairstyles. I observed that everyone's unique features had a lot to do with what color and cut looked best on them. Whether I was correct or not, I thoroughly enjoyed envisioning ways in which I would do their hair differently.

My parents' divorce when I was in 7th grade was hard on me, as was my mom's relocation to Iowa after I graduated from college. But my love and passion for hair and art kept me going through the ups and downs of growing up.

When my feelings were bottled up inside, I was able to express myself in drawing, painting, creating, or styling hair. Art was always my outlet. I quickly learned that it was my way of dealing with my emotions, as I was a sensitive child and young woman, and just wanted everyone around me to be happy. I did everything in my power to help those who were not happy. I have always yearned to help others.

In high school and college, I was friends with everyone. I was the girl cutting and styling hair for fun. In high school, my brother's friends would ask me to do their hair instead of going to their regular hairdressers or barbers. Then, in college, I practiced hair on all the girls in my dorm room. Soon enough, I was making a little side money just doing my friends' and friends of friends' hair. At this point, I'd had no training, but I just kind of went with it, so glad that I could make others happy! Doing hair has always come naturally to me. The best part is, I thoroughly enjoy it. It feels good to make others feel good about themselves.

I graduated from the University of Vermont in 2001 with an elementary education degree and a minor in psychology. I loved working with children, but it was obvious to everyone and myself, that my true passion and gift was hair.

So, why didn't I just go to cosmetology school directly after graduating from high school? To be honest, I felt the normal pressure to get a college degree.

While part of me wished I had gone to hair school right after high school, I am actually very grateful and thankful for the higher education I received. It's certainly been beneficial to me in opening my own business, and in how I run my salon.

My psychology education has been very handy when working with the public. Having an understanding of why people act or react a certain way or why they might feel insecure is a huge asset in the service industry.

Having some psychology knowledge also has helped me better understand how to react to many situations behind the chair. As many of you know, we stylists also act as therapists at times. Clients share a lot of their personal lives with us. For many, it is a very sacred relationship.

My education degree has helped me as I instruct other stylists and former employees on cutting and coloring techniques. I've been blessed with extreme patience, and one goal always has been to help other stylists think creatively, while helping them discover their strengths. While I consider myself an inspiring and compassionate educator, I've learned that I cannot teach passion – it needs to be embedded within you.

After graduating from Pivot Point International Cosmetology School near Chicago in 2002, I started my very first job doing children's hair in the Chicago suburbs. How perfect! I got to use my elementary education degree while practicing my true passion.

Working at a salon for children, I quickly realized that kids move fast, and I had only a limited amount of time. Being a perfectionist, I wanted to find a way in which no child would leave my chair with uneven hair. My cuts had to look flawless, because they were a reflection of my work. They had my name on them!

Dry cutting has always made perfect sense for me. I was able to explore my natural tendency to cut dry while working on children. First of all, kids hate being sprayed with water. So, I steered away from using water to avoid screaming and an unhappy experience for the child. Secondly, I could see what I was doing when the hair was dry; I could see where I was cutting.

The Jen-uine Dry Cut

How many times have you seen a child's haircut look uneven, or cut too short? By cutting dry, I was able to avoid taking off too much, and to add layers more efficiently. I was able to give straight bangs, or wispy bangs, depending on the desired look.

Oh, and how about those cowlicks that I could only see sticking up when they were dry? Cutting dry allowed me to not cut the cowlick too short. It also let me work with the cowlick and not against it. I could actually shape the cowlick in a way so that it would not stick up and would blend much better with the overall design.

Also, when cutting dry, I got more time to shape. I am sure we all know that most kids do not love getting their hair cut and rarely sit still. Sometimes, a lollipop and a balloon are not enough. Not using water resulted in less crying, and more cut time.

Soon the children's parents realized that there was something special about this dry cutting technique, and they started making appointments for themselves. I began providing dry cuts for the whole family. This is when I just knew that I was on to something. Everyone else around me cut wet. Others would question my approach with dry cutting, and I would reply, "it just makes sense to me; we do not walk around with our hair wet". I would explain that I could actually see what I was doing. I want to make it clear that it is not my intent to denounce or criticize a wet cut. I know my version of a dry cut (and dry cutting in general) may not be for everyone.

I have always only cut dry, and I am grateful that the salons in which I worked embraced my style and did not force me to cut hair wet. Between the consultation and cut, each client visit took well over an hour. I didn't focus on just my paycheck; but as an opportunity to create art fueled by my desire to perfect each and every head of hair.

A turning point for me was landing a job at an upscale salon outside of Chicago. This is where I met Patty McGuire, one of the salon managers. She is a true artist who trained me primarily in color. I loved watching her do hair, and she always took time to answer my questions.

Patty helped me to recognize that my unique approach to doing hair was a gift and encouraged me to embrace it. Not only did she understand me, she motivated me to tap into my creativity and certainly boosted my confidence. Patty allowed me to be me, and because she did not require me to work just like the majority of the other stylists, I learned that being different was okay.

Most importantly, Patty helped me acknowledge and accept what I already intuitively knew: We are all artists, and we all have our own way of doing things. Once Patty started sending clients my way, their response was overwhelmingly positive. I am forever grateful to have had her as a mentor. She gave me what I needed - inspiration, assurance, and motivation.

Opening My Salon: "The Artistic Edge"

Recognizing that my artistry ("artistic edge") has been with me throughout my life, I knew I had to create my own environment. The easiest way to do so was to open my own salon at age 25, in a northwest suburb of Chicago. The business moved with me as I relocated numerous times to four different states.

The name "The Artistic Edge" made perfect sense because it described me and how I worked. Embracing myself as an artist, while recognizing that I had a little bit of an "edge," different from other stylists, helped me to create this name.

Hair is my inner spirit or soul. By opening my own salon, I was able to set its tone, and to explore the most efficient ways to help others feel better about themselves. In return, this made me feel good, and gave me an undeniable purpose.

I've always found myself more interested in perfecting my work, rather than in selling products or making a huge commission. I could not multitask on two or three clients at once, nor did I want to. I worked best when it was just me and my client, with no external energies or interruptions.

My philosophy and meticulous approach did not align with the time-oriented, profit-driven approach which we were taught in school.

As doing hair has always been embedded in my soul, so has the art of dry cutting. It made more sense to look at my "canvas" as a whole. It came naturally to me to tackle my sculpture based on what the hair was doing, and how it was acting.

And Who Are YOU?

Before I delve more into the art of dry cutting, and why I believe every stylist should at least give it a try, let's take a look at who you are.

- You are a stylist already established in the industry who is open to learning new techniques. Maybe you enjoy dry cutting at the end of a traditional wet cut, and you want to learn more about this cutting-edge technique. You are passionate about what you do, and you want to find a way in which every client who sits in your chair leaves happy.

- Maybe you work at a busier salon, and you are kept on a strict schedule. You feel as though you are not getting enough time to perfect your work, and you are not completely satisfied with the outcome because you are feeling rushed.

- Maybe you work more slowly, and find it impossible to do a cut in 30 minutes or you crave a more private setting or more of a "drama-free" atmosphere in which to work. Most importantly, you want to do the best work that you can do and you want to grow as a stylist. You are searching for different ways to achieve this. You know that the techniques you've learned in school are just the beginning, and there is so much more out there for you to attain. You yearn to help others while doing your craft and want to find an approach that works best for you to achieve this end goal.

- You are a stylist-in-training who feels that there is something more than what you are learning from the textbooks. Maybe cutting wet does not click with you, or you are more of an abstract thinker than others in your class. You know you are an artist, and you are searching for the fuel that ignites your enthusiasm for doing hair. Do not give up now, because the possibilities are endless. You do not have to do hair exactly how you are taught in school. Keep searching, and you will find the approaches and cutting methods which work best for you.

- You might be thinking of going to cosmetology school, but are unsure if this is the right step for you. You feel hesitant because of what you think being in the hair industry entails. This book is a wonderful place for you to start, because it will open your mind to possibilities that not many talk about: approaches and techniques that you did not even know existed.

As hairdressers, one of our basic roles is to make others feel better about themselves and to give them looks that will give them a lift. Being a hairdresser is actually a very challenging job, which includes a lot of responsibilities. Some think it is an easy job, and this could not be farther from the truth. We need a wide range of competencies such as math, chemistry, time management, people skills, communication and listening skills, and many more – in addition to our craft.

And we all need the support I was so fortunate to get from my mentor. Especially if we are fueled with passion, sometimes the only thing stopping us is a lack of confidence. We need encouragement, and the understanding that a non-traditional approach is just fine.

That is what sets us apart as artists. Wouldn't hair be boring if we all did the same technique? I encourage you to "do you" behind the chair. Be the unique artist that you are deep inside. While considering the facts and knowledge that you gained in school, try and look at your next cut without labels.

Let your creativity take over and generate your vision. Do not worry about the "type" of haircut you are doing; rather try focusing on making your vision come to life on whomever is in your chair.

Wet Cutting vs. Dry Cutting: The Major Differences

Wet hair truly is much easier to cut because the strands group together: one of the reasons why it is so much faster. You are following a system provided for you in school with definitions of the types of cuts you are doing. While this technique is successful for so many, it is just not for me. My cuts have to connect, flow, and naturally work. I cannot envision that happening if I cut wet.

Wet cutting is what almost everyone knows. As you learned from the cosmetology textbooks, there are four types of cuts:

1. The 0° haircut is also known as the "Blunt" or "Bob" cut.
2. The 45° cut is also known as the "Wedge".
3. The 90° cut is also known as the "Layered" haircut.
4. The 180° cut is also known as the "Shag" or the "Reverse Elevation".

These four cuts specifically, and wet cutting in general, are all about strict sectioning, elevation, lines, graduation, and control. With a wet cut, the formulas used simply do not accommodate for the way the hair *really* looks.

Wet cutting is a technique in which the client comes in and gets their hair washed, cut, and then styled. As you know, the wash and blow dry take time. This leaves very little room for the cutting process, especially if you have only 45 minutes (or sometimes less) to do it all.

Do you ever notice how with a traditional wet haircut, you sometimes dry your client's hair, and then go back over it again with the scissors, trimming here and there? You are cutting the pieces that were not accounted for when the hair was wet. Doing it dry to begin with eliminates the need for this "fixer work." It makes your job so much easier to cut it dry from the beginning. You will find the whole cut flows more smoothly from start to finish.

Shaping and trimming the hair after doing a wash, wet cut, and blow-dry is not a true organic dry cut. It is more like a finishing touch. A true dry haircut is much more complex than a traditional wet cut.

So What, Exactly, is a Dry Cut?

We do not wear our hair wet, so why would we cut it wet?

Dry cutting takes place when the stylist cuts the hair when it is dry, and in its natural state. While it has been around for a while, dry cutting is a technique that is becoming increasingly more popular, especially in the past few years.

A true dry cut is not taught in the cosmetology schools or textbooks. It is merely touched upon as a suggestion to do a little dry cutting after a traditional wash, wet cut, and blow-dry. This finishing touch is more of a saving grace when doing wet cuts, because you can quickly clean up the pieces that were missed. Dry cutting at the end for two minutes is a quick attempt to fix problems that were not taken into account when the hair was cut wet. This is very different from a true dry cut.

My personal definition of a dry cut is when you dry cut your client's hair in its true organic state from beginning to end, no water necessary. I've seen various approaches to dry cutting. A dry cut can take place as soon as your client sits in the chair (before washing), or after you've washed and dried the hair. My approach to dry cutting is a little different, and I have not seen many stylists work this way. I ask my client to come in with hair freshly washed, and air dried. This way, my client's hair has not been pulled or stretched from a brush, dryer, or iron. This allows me to see all problem areas. Instead of spending time washing and drying the hair, I can do a thorough consultation and cut. I can spend the entire time sculpting and detailing, which results in an easy-to-style and lasting cut. The more details added and problem areas addressed (which involves time) can be the difference between a good cut and a phenomenal cut.

When I opened my salon in Schaumburg, Illinois in 2004, dry cutting was scarce and hard to find. While some wonderful artists, such as the previously mentioned John Sahag (Inventor of the Dry Cut), had been dry cutting for years, and Chicago was very advanced with hair, many had not yet heard of dry cutting.

But now, the word is spreading about this top-notch technique.

Twelve Reasons Why Dry is Better

1. **Getting your haircut dry produces fewer surprises and therefore less anxiety.** Wet cutting and anxious clients are not a good combination. There are way too many unknowns. We want to avoid those "uh-oh" moments in the mirror when the client gets home and attempts to style their hair themselves. For nervous clients, when their hair is wet, they have no idea what is happening, and what it is going to look like, until the appointment is over.

   In a sense, **wet hair can "lie" while dry hair presents "the truth".** With a dry cut, there is no need to wait to dry and style your client's hair to see if they like the length or movement. Your client will see it as it is happening. A beautiful blow dry and style at the end does not give your client a true picture of how it will look the next day. When they go to do it themselves, they will not be able to achieve the same look, which then leads to disappointment. Cutting dry eliminates any shock factor for the present moment, for the next day, and after.

2. **When hair is dry, you can see and feel weight lines,** so you can remove necessary bulk more accurately. Dry hair reveals thicker areas

throughout the hair that need attention. How many times does a client complain about heavy ledges or steps in their hair? Most clients come in to get their haircut because "it feels heavy," or "it's not doing anything," or "it needs more volume," or "there is no shape".

Dry cutting can address all of these woes. Weight lines not accounted for when hair is cut wet can result in hard ledges. Cuts should flow, unless the cut calls for an intentional shelf or weight line. Blending is more difficult when the hair is wet, and you cannot see the full composition of each section let alone each individual strand. So, how can you effectively blend what you cannot see?

Think about a traditional fade. Clipper cutting is best done on dry hair because wet hair tends to move away from the clipper blades as it moves through the hair. Therefore, when the hair is wet, you will most likely have to go over the same places again and again with the clippers to get it all. Try doing fades dry – you will be able to see exactly where you need to transition or debulk better. Fading is a whole new world when you cut dry. **It is seamless.**

3. **When hair is wet, it is weighed down by water and the hair clumps together, so it is harder to see where you are cutting.** Cowlicks,

curl patterns, waves, weight lines, and bulk all get lost when the hair is wet. The weight of the water pulls the hair down. The moisture of the water flattens curls and waves and minimizes thickness.

When the hair clumps together, the hair might be cut in the wrong place, causing it to actually stick out in odd areas. We can all remember a time or two in our career that this happened. Please never cut curly hair unless it is dry. Every strand of hair has its own unique identity, and a well-shaped cut can be achieved only if this uniqueness is taken into account. We do not walk around with our hair wet, so why would we cut it while it's wet? **Doesn't it make more sense to cut the hair in the state in which we wear it?**

4. **Dry cutting is an abstract way of cutting with more focus on the overall shape.** Wet hair cutting is very focused on partings and sectioning. It's hard to see the benefit of making a perfect parting (or spending so much energy on partings) when what really matters is the end result. Of course, you section the hair when dry cutting, especially with thick hair, but you don't need to obsess over sectioning the hair in a certain way. During a dry cut, you are spending a great deal of time **sculpting and carving your sculpture instead of obsessing over partings.**

5. **With a dry cut, your clients can go much longer until their next cut because the shape lasts!** Why? Sculpting dry allows you to add detail work much more efficiently. The more detailed work and carving you can do allows for a much more flowing shape. A thorough cut that has addressed all problem areas (because you can see them) will allow the shape to last. As we know, **something that is done right from the beginning will last longer than something not done thoroughly and carefully.**

6. **Hair shrinks up to 50% when it dries** because the water weighs down the true integrity of the hair. Hair will shorten and look totally different when it's dry. Curly and wavy hair that is stretched when wet results in an unpredictable cut.

Consider this scenario: a client with curly hair comes in and says she wants "just a trim" (less than 2 inches taken off). You proceed to cut 2 inches off when the hair is wet, and it ends up much shorter with random pieces that are longer than others. Why does this happen? You are stretching wet curly and wavy hair and cutting it one length. It is truly impossible to know how each curl is going to dry. So you will have an uneven, unprecedented cut. With a dry cut, there is **no shrinkage, no hidden surprises!**

7. **Dry hair reveals split ends which wet hair will mask.** Dry cutting allows you to see exactly what needs attention and where. When hair is wet, you cannot see the split ends or flyaways. It is so much harder to see damaged areas when hair is wet. Why is this so? The split ends are also hidden from moisture. And wet hair masks split ends that are present on the surface. Are you familiar with the term "hair dusting", also referred to as "surface cutting"? By seeing all the frizzy or frayed ends when the hair is dry (on the ends of the formation and all throughout the hair), you effectively can remove this breakage. **The end result is a much smoother and healthier cut that will hold its shape longer.**

8. **Dry cutting causes less damage to the hair.** Wet hair is fragile and elastic. Wet hair actually can be prone to snapping or splitting when it is combed over and over. Cutting it wet can cause the ends to fray. Hair that is not frayed is healthier hair. **When held down by gravity (water), the hair cannot breathe or move.** The hair needs to be able to breathe to ensure movement and volume. When hair is dry, you can create much more body because you can see where the hair needs texture and lift.

9. **Dry cutting allows you to be extremely specific in your composition.** When you are wet

cutting, you are following a formula, and that simply cannot work for all hair types. Keep in mind that everyone's head has differing formations all over. This means the right side is not the same as the left side. Someone might have more curls on the left side or a cowlick on the right. Not only is each person's head of hair unique, but the individual strands vary as well. Dry cutting takes all of these variants into account.

Cutting dry provides a **cause and an effect**; each time you cut, you will see a reaction. You can immediately see how the hair responds. This is so beneficial in many ways – especially accuracy.

10. **Dry cutting ensures you will not cut the hair too short.** This applies to all hair types, not just those with curls. **Wet hair appears longer** because it is being stretched. Consider how many times your clients have cut their own bangs at home, and they ended up too short. This happens because they are cutting their bangs wet. They're not accounting for cowlicks which usually exist in the bangs area.

11. **A dry cut is a good option for people who do minimal styling.** Dry cutting provides a style that your clients can easily do themselves. Since the shape is perfected, clients do not need to spend

much time styling their hair. After getting a dry cut, the client might not yearn for someone else to style their hair (or to come in for a wash, blow-dry, and style). They find it easier to do it themselves. They will feel happy with their hair and see what their hair can actually **do on its own**.

12. **When cutting dry, what you see is what you get.** You and your client can watch the shape unfold as you cut!

Why Does Dry Cutting Take Longer?

Wet cutting takes much less time because when hair is wet, strands group together, making it faster to cut. It lays flat, stays in one place, and sticks together. While this is a quicker way to cut, it does not account for each individual strand and what each strand does naturally.

The technique for shaping hair dry is detailed and delicate because each strand is cut individually. Therefore, it is time-consuming. One needs to be detail-oriented and to have a great deal of patience (and training) in order to cut dry.

When the hair is dry, **everything** is visible and evident:
- **Every split end.**
- **Every cowlick and swirl.**
- **Every wave.**
- **Every problem that needs de-bulking, texture, or layers.**

Dry cutting can address all of these problem areas, and it takes more time, energy, and focus because nothing is hidden from moisture.

A common question is: "I have very thin, limp, and fine hair. I want to keep my length, so is there anything you can do to make it look thicker"?

So many women want to keep their length and have more volume and movement. They don't want to have to always put their long hair up because it "will not do anything".

Many first-time clients struggle with this issue. Usually, they've been told by other hair stylists that it is not possible without taking length off. As a result, they end up with a much shorter cut. Sometimes, they just end up with a simple trim on the ends.

Here is just another way dry cutting comes to the rescue. When the hair is dry, you can see every split end, not only on the ends of the hair, but also the flyaways on the surface of the hair. Taking this hair off will give your client healthier hair. Healthier hair means more body and shape.

To conserve the length, you are able to take off only the split ends, nothing more than absolutely necessary. You can see where to add texture or add layers to give the client's hair lift and character. You also can create blended layers and make sure there are no steps (or bulk) in the layers. These are referred to as "cascading layers", and it results in a beautiful transition. You also can add texture and face-framing layers, all while maintaining the client's long length. It's amazing what a thorough cut will do. Your client's long hair will have a shape they did not even know was possible.

The Jen-uine Dry Cut

How much time does a dry cut take? You begin with an abstract picture in mind. While not every cut takes as long, it just is not possible to get a good (and lasting) haircut in 15 or 30 minutes of cut time.

Help your clients understand why they'll pay more for dry cutting

If you want to try dry cutting, be prepared to charge more and to help your clients understand why. Since dry cutting takes longer, this means fewer appointments in your workday. I book out at least an hour of cut time, usually an hour and a half to be safe (especially for new clients). Dry cutting is laborious, so you can and should charge more for your time. And just as other professionals charge for their expertise and special training, we should charge not only for our time, but for our creativity.

In addition to the fact that it takes much longer:

- **It requires more training.** As stylists, we pay for this on our own. The cost of these classes is more than usual because there are not as many stylists who practice dry cutting. When you seek out training, choose your teacher carefully. Check with your local cosmetology schools and ask if they know of anyone certified in dry cutting. Or you can call reputable salons who specialize in dry cutting and ask if any of their stylists teach this specialized technique. Finding someone to teach you is difficult – which is one of the reasons I wrote this book.

- **Each cut is customized for that one client.** You are creating based on his/her type of hair, face shape, and desired look. You simply cannot get a tailored cut from a wet cut.

- **The time you spend cutting includes just you and them.** They have your undivided attention. Many clients will appreciate this special attention and gladly will pay more just to have you working on them and not multitasking. You can emphasize to clients how special and rare this is; to have a stylist spending more than an hour sculpting and creating only on their canvas.

- **There are no hidden surprises.** The certainty that comes with a dry cut is worth a lot to clients.

- **The shape will last longer.** The amount of detailing that can be done when shaping dry softens hard lines and prevents the look from becoming unruly in the grow out process. There is a much longer grow-out time, hence fewer trips to the salon. Let's do the math. If a wet cut costs $50 (with the client returning every 4 to 6 weeks), the client would be paying $400-$600/year. Yet, if a dry cut is $100 (double the price, with the client returning every 10 to 18 weeks), clients would be paying $300-$500/year. So, in the long run the client is actually saving money.

- **Dry cutting shears cost more.** Cutting dry can be rough on our tools. We use specialized shears that will provide a much cleaner cut, and that do not fray hair ends. You also must have a few pairs of longer shears, so that you can do deep point notching (which you want to do only on dry hair).

- **Sharpening costs can add up quickly.** Even with an expensive pair of dry cutting shears, dry hair can dull your shears. With high end shears comes high maintenance. You must sharpen your shears very often. This way, you can ensure they provide a very clean cut on the ends of the hair.

- **Your client will not need to spend as much on products or equipment.** With the comprehensive work done with dry cuts, the hair will move on its own. A dry cut with natural lift, movement, and shape means not as much need for root lifters, mousse, sea salt sprays, gels, and texturizing sprays. Ditto for round brushes, flat irons, or curling irons, the cost of which can really add up. Your client will be amazed to find their hair looks good without fuss and extra money spent.

- **Clients will save a lot of time in the morning.** Time is money. The less time your clients spend on their hair means more time for family, work, exercise, activities, and life.

The Jen-uine Dry Cut

During the first five or so years of running my own business, I was so scared to charge more than the going rate for a wash, cut, and blow dry. I got busy fast, and my demand was high. I was booked out for months, had a waiting list, and could not find reliable employees.

Believe it or not, it was my clients who actually were encouraging me to charge more. My clients saw the value in my way of cutting. My cuts were different. My clients loved being the only client. They always left happy. No one else offered anything like this in the area. They were also shocked how long they could go in between haircuts. They valued my worth.

So, while when you first get started, you might not be aware of your value, it soon will become increasingly clear how special you are based on your clients' reactions. That, in itself, will give you the confidence to charge more.

Remember, your customers have chosen to come to you for a reason. They have many options as to where to go for their hair services. Once you are confident that you are charging what you are worth, your clients will understand why this technique is so special. It is customized for them. **Who isn't willing to pay more for something created just for them?**

How is Dry Cutting Beneficial to Those with Extensions or Color?

How many times have you seen someone in a salon, or out on a Saturday night, where their extensions were not blended? It is just so obvious that you want to get your scissors out and help!

No one really wants others to know they are wearing extensions. Or, at least, they do not want it to be the first thing someone notices. This is just another example where dry cutting can help. When hair is dry, you can see demarcation lines and where blending is necessary. Many times, the colors of the extensions do not match the color of the real hair. This color differentiation can be so obvious. Wet hair can mask the true color of the hair. This is why we tell our clients to wait to see the true color until it is dry. It is next to impossible to efficiently blend the two colors while wet cutting.

Doing it dry is a whole different story. You can texturize and notch where the colors meet, and help them to blend into one another.

Also, the extension hair rarely has the same texture and shine as the client's natural hair. Usually, the extension hair is shinier and smoother, and that's difficult to see when the hair is wet. You usually do not want to cut into the client's real hair, so when it's dry, you can notch into the extension hair to help blend the two textures. You can create an unbroken progression from natural to extension hair.

I absolutely love color! Many clients do not need to get their hair colored as often with dry cuts. When sculpting hair dry, you can see where the hair is unhealthy.

Usually, faded or dulled color goes along with dry hair and split ends. By addressing these problems, you can transform the hair into healthier hair. When hair is healthy and not frayed, the color looks fresher and brighter.

Why Don't More Hairdressers Dry Cut?

Some of these benefits to the client may be impediments to the hairdresser:

- **It takes longer.** This means spending a long time with just one client. Some hairdressers do not like this approach. You may work best with one client after another, and might lose your focus during a dry cut. We all work differently.

- **It is extremely detail-oriented and takes intense focus.** Perhaps it is too detailed, or too abstract for you. Maybe you work better with a system. It's not wrong. It's how we are taught in school.

- **There is an extra cost of maintaining shears.** As mentioned above, dry cutting shears cost a lot and need to be sharpened frequently because dry cutting is harder on the shears.

- **True dry cutting is not taught in school.** Sure, doing a little dry cutting at the end of a cut is touched upon in school. Detail work at the end is not a true dry cut. Imagine that you do not need to go back at the end when you are finished sculpting. When dry cutting, you are able to address every detail during the cutting process from beginning to end. If you haven't learned the process, you cannot implement it.

- **You will need to get further education.** You will need to take a dry cutting class – at your own expense – if you want to start practicing this cutting-edge technique. You also will need to practice because it needs to *feel* right to be *done* right, and that may or may not resonate with you. Or you may decide to dry cut some clients, while wet cutting others.

Cutting dry is different, and it may just be the difference between liking what you do and loving what you do. So I am going to share my personal journey in the art of dry cutting, and I hope you will grow to love it too.

Introducing:
The JEN-UINE DRY CUT™!

"How To Be A Cut Above The Rest"

*"When I entered the hair industry, I realized that I was different from my colleagues in many ways. Not only did I work more slowly, but I was not interested in upselling clients or selling products for commission. I was most interested in a perfect and thorough cut. I found my calling in what I have named **THE JEN-UINE DRY CUT**™, and doing hair has been effortless since."*

The Jen-uine Dry Cut™: Is it for you?

Before I describe **THE JEN-UINE DRY CUT**™ in more detail, please take a look at these questions. If you can answer "yes" to one or more, I truly believe my approach will resonate with you. Consider:

- Do you like to look **outside the box** and consider the overall picture?

- Do you yearn to **make others feel better about themselves**?

- Do you have a **strong intuition,** and feel comfortable following your gut?

- Are you **naturally sensitive** to others?

- Are you a perfectionist and/or **detail-oriented**?

- Do you always **strive for 100% client satisfaction**, no matter the outside circumstances?

- Are you ready to **explore different ways of cutting/styling/coloring** outside of the school textbook?

- Are you an **abstract thinker**?

- Do you prefer to **take your time**, instead of rushing to get to the next client?

- Do you work better when you are **not under time pressure**?

- Do you find yourself **able to visualize the desired look** before you begin cutting?

- Do you really **"get into" your work**, and not get easily distracted?

- Are you 100% focused (or want to be) on just the **one client in your chair**?

- Are you usually able to **pinpoint the look your client is seeking**?

- Does **finding the best look for the client's face and lifestyle** entice you?

- Do you prefer an **extensive consultation**?

- Are you able to work on **someone's hair (strictly sculpting) for at least an hour**?

- Are you **sensitive to negative energy**, and wish that you could control the environment in which you do hair?

- Do you have **passion stirring within you,** but maybe have not found the approach that works best for you?

- Are you interested in competing only with yourself, and **being the best stylist you can be**, rather than focusing on competing with others?

- Are you able to stay **present in the moment**, and what is happening right now?

Should any of these questions pique your interest, you likely will enjoy learning about the methods which have worked so well for me.

What is The Jen-uine Dry Cut™?

THE JEN-UINE DRY CUT™ is not just simply my version of a dry cut. It is also an approach and a way of working from beginning to end that taps into your ability as an artist, while you approach your gift with integrity and sincerity.

It is a well-thought-out process, focusing on only one client at a time. It is a detailed approach, in which each client who sits in the chair leaves satisfied.

It is a true effort to make sure each and every client I see genuinely loves his or her hair.

As a naturally sensitive individual, I am able to pick up on how the client in my chair is feeling. Intuition is such a valuable tool, which we each have. Most of us work with our gut feeling, without even knowing it. So I encourage you to be aware of and trust your instincts.

Hair is art. You are the artist. You have the opportunity to provide unique cuts for your clients. Just as a painter has a palette and creates a beautiful masterpiece that cannot be replicated, so do you. Your canvas is as unique as the result.

My vision – sometimes unexplainable – is a formation and creation based on the consultation, the client's (natural) hair, and the desired result. This is the essence of **THE JEN-UINE DRY CUT™**.

The difference between a "just-okay" cut and a phenomenal cut is the details and the time spent sculpting every piece of hair. Practicing **THE JEN-UINE DRY CUT**™ is all about details. You will be tapping into your passion for creating, while being electrified and inspired by your intuition.

Did you know that hair is one of the top three features mentioned when describing another person aesthetically? Think about it: whenever describing what someone looks like, you almost always say, "she has long, blonde hair", or "he has short, curly hair". You might not even remember his or her name, but you will remember what their hair looked like. Hair creates a first impression. Hair is a key component of self-expression.

As hairdressers, we have such a rewarding job, where we are given the chance to help others feel better about their appearance and themselves. Having good hair boosts confidence. While everyone's interpretation of "good hair"' is different, we stylists should do whatever it takes to make that one client in our chair realize their personal definition of "good hair". Hair is the one thing we can change about our physical appearance that does not have to be permanent.

Why did you choose to become a hairdresser? Most of us would say, at least in part, that we have a gift for taking care of others. It is rewarding for me to know that I've helped another person. I want to make them genuinely smile, boost their confidence, and love their hair as an expression of who they are.

The right cut can be a reflection of the client's inner self. It is liberating when you find the right cut. So many of my clients come back for their next cut telling me that they now can easily style their hair for the first time ever.

To do **THE JEN-UINE DRY CUT**™, you must be living in the moment. This way, you are responding to what is unfolding directly in front of you.

It is so important for us to be present for each and every client. If you follow this approach, I promise you will find this much easier to do.

25 Essential Elements of The Jen-uine Dry Cut™

Setting you up to be successful behind the chair - every time!

1. Create a "zen" environment for you and for your client.

> *"Ideas just flow much better when there are no outside interruptions. I don't know about you, but I crave an atmosphere where there is no drama. For me, the only way to create the environment I wanted was to open my own salon, where I could set the energy, the tone, and the atmosphere."*

All artists need a relaxed environment when doing their craft, whether it is painting, pottery, sketching, photography, or cutting hair. Instead of paintbrushes or pencils, our tools are our hands and shears.

If you need a more relaxed surrounding, you do not necessarily need to open your own salon. Consider how you can be more in charge of the environment in which you work. This means no outside interference. Many salon managers and salon owners will provide you with a more private space for you to work. You might just need to ask.

You also have the option to rent a private suite. This is a great way for you to work by yourself, while creating a name for yourself.

So many people are in a rush these days. Everywhere you go, whether to the grocery store, gas station, or on the highway, people are in a hurry. Rushing is not relaxing. I realized early on that the number one reason most people go to the salon is to relax, to be pampered, and to feel better than when they came in. Most of us do not like "hustle and bustle" when trying to relax.

Your clients will notice and appreciate the drama-free environment you are providing. They will want to come back to this "at-ease" environment, where they feel so special. **Doing amazing work is awesome, and the way in which you treat your client is just as important.**

2. **THE JEN-uine DRY CUT™ is a cut for all!**

"I cut all clients' hair dry, not one exception."

Dry cutting can be done on any hair type: straight, curly, wavy, extra curly, coarse, fine, thin, or thick. Others who specialize in the art of dry cutting might choose to dry cut only curly and wavy hair. Again, this is what makes us distinctive as artists. It is up to you how you want to deliver your gift of doing hair.

Look at your cuts without rigid labels. No two people are alike, just as curl patterns, cowlicks, and texture are all different on each individual in your chair. How can we label cuts when everyone's hair is so different? Look at your canvas as a whole and think abstractly in order to tailor your sculptures. To give each client the best possible cut, you have to base the shaping on what the hair is doing. Do so while taking into consideration symmetry, texture, and head shape.

Without labels, you have complete creative and artistic freedom. When given the chance to create without instructions, many artists do their best work. You will be amazed as you experience this.

3. Help clients prepare for their dry cut.

> *"I always tell my clients to come to see me with their hair in its natural state with as little product as possible. This way, I am able to observe and feel their hair in its organic condition."*

It's best when clients wash their hair and let it air dry. This allows you to see exactly how their hair falls without masking any of its natural integrity.

Washing all the dirt and hair products from the hair also helps you get a better idea about the health of the hair and where you will be sculpting. With respect to time, it is not realistic for you to wash a client's hair and then let it air dry before their cut. This is why it's best to have them do it a couple of hours before arriving. **Seeing the hair in its pure state is key**, so that all issues can be observed and addressed.

4. The consultation: the single most important part of the appointment!

> *"I will not begin my creation until this trust is established, and that requires good communication. Hair is a very intimate part of a person's life, and it is our job to help each client feel better about themselves as a result of their hair."*

THE JEN-UINE DRY CUT™ begins with a thorough, extensive consultation in which communication, honesty, and intuition are all key components.

Building a friendly and authentic relationship with the client from the start is important. Always maintain casual eye contact when appropriate. This is the allotted time to connect with the client and to set expectations for their "hair journey". Trust is built this way. This time cannot be rushed in order for it to flow naturally.

Sometimes, people are unable to articulate their true desires verbally, so it's necessary to rely on intuition to sense their desires, fears, and comfort zones. Asking questions helps to get a feel of what the client is or is not emotionally ready for.

Most clients are looking for a complimentary, sometimes different, appealing cut on which they don't have to spend much time. Time is an important factor, since most everyone has a busy schedule and they not only want, but need, a look that takes less time.

The key is recognizing the look they crave, and then creating that look to the best of our abilities. We owe it to our clients, who have put their trust in us, to honor their requests while not compromising our integrity and skills.

Since some clients have never heard of a dry cut, or if they have, don't fully understand the approach, it's important to explain the technique at the beginning of the consultation. Usually, they are excited to try something different.

Having confidence in what you are offering is so important. I find that clients love to be educated about how my approach is different. This way, they know what to expect and will believe in what you are offering because you are exuding confidence in your craft. So, please make sure you understand this concept and feel assured before offering it to your clients.

It's also important to fully explain what to expect during and after their visit, and how a thorough consultation will help achieve an exceptional end result. Assuring your client that you will do all you can to make sure he or she is satisfied is very calming.

Is it a good idea for clients to bring in photos of what they want? While photos can be a good start, some clients bring a photo from a magazine of what they *think* they want. They see a look on a model and now want this same style. They might not be considering their unique face shape, skin complexion, or texture of hair. It is part of our job to be honest about whether we can deliver the desired outcome in comparison to the magazine or internet photo.

Far too many stylists say "yes" to their client's wishes without communicating their expert advice. While a well-intended effort to please, this will just result in a disappointed or unhappy client, who may not book with you again. We need to be honest and genuine, and not mislead them and/or get their hopes up. Sometimes, these desired looks are just unrealistic, and it's better that the client know and understand that from the start.

Your clients also may be heavily influenced by the people around them: their peers, or even their spouses. It's vital that you determine what *they* want and what will bring satisfaction.

Ask the key questions and find the answers to determine what will make them – not others around them – happy.

The person in your chair is the one who will be living with his or her new look every day.

As artists, we also must be careful not to give clients a look that *we* want for them. We certainly can give suggestions and our professional opinion, but simply doing what we think will look good will not always leave the client satisfied and happy.

Seeing the hair dry and undisguised (with no product) during the consultation is key to getting good results. When clients arrive with their hair freshly washed and air dried, **nothing is masking or interfering with the way their hair naturally acts**.

With a good consultation, the cut will unfold naturally. You will avoid the "fixer" appointment the next day in between your already-booked schedule.

During the consultation, **always show how many inches you are taking off**. This will work only on dry hair because, as previously emphasized, wet hair shrinks. Having someone show us their idea of what four inches off looks like on wet hair is almost useless.

> *"A typical scenario in my salon: A client says she wants about five inches cut off, but my gut is telling me she's not ready. So I ask her to show me her idea of five inches, because almost always, the client's*

perception is much less than our definition of five inches. Even though my client was saying she wanted a shorter cut, I felt that what she really wanted was more volume, lift, and character. Layering and adding texture would give her the look she wanted. She desired more movement, but didn't know this was possible by adding blended layers. So, I followed my intuition and asked the right questions. I'm so glad I listened closely to my client's words while also listening to my instinct. She would not have been happy with a shorter cut. We discovered together that longer hair gives her confidence."

When there is open communication, the entire process flows instead of feeling forced. It's easy to feel if the client trusts me and is fully comfortable. This connection often happens within the first few minutes of the consultation because they can tell that I am going to take my time, and most importantly, that I truly care.

Here are some questions to ask during the consultation:

- What do you **like about your hair**?

- What do you wish you could **change about your hair**?

- How do you feel about the **condition of your hair**?

- Do you feel **ready for a change**?

- What is your **biggest challenge** with your hair?

- How **often do you shampoo**?

- How much time do you spend **doing your hair**?

- Do you want to spend **less time on styling**?

- What are you **hoping to achieve** with your hair today?

- What have you done in the **past that you liked or disliked**?

- Is **maintaining your length a priority**?

- Do you **wear your hair different ways** (i.e., curly, straight, wavy), or do you prefer to wear it just one way?

- Is there a look you **WANT to do but are scared to do**?

- In your opinion, what is your **"perfect" hair day**?

- Do you have a **picture of yourself** when you loved your hair?

Some questions just for the "curly girls":

- Do you want a **more rounded look or more height**?

- Do you want the curls to **frame your face**?

- Do you want to **stay away from a triangular shape**?

(Many clients with curly hair end up with this unfortunate shape because not enough layers or texture are added on the sides and top. So the heaviness is at the ends, which does not allow the rest of the hair to breathe. This pulls the hair down and creates a triangular shape where all of the weight sits at the bottom).

- Do you need to be able **to pull your hair up**?

- How do you **wear your curls** (down, half up, or in a clip) most often?

- Do you find yourself **always putting your hair up** because you do not like the overall shape?

- Do you feel as though you ever have **found a look, which embraced your curls**, that you were comfortable with?

- Do you want to **enhance your curls**?

- What **products do you use** when styling your curls?

- Would you **like to use less product** and avoid that crunchy look?

- Do you straighten your hair often because you **do not know what to do with your natural curls**?

5. After consulting and before picking up the shears, you will have a clear vision.

> *"I always have a clear vision of what I want to achieve before I start cutting."*

Once you've encompassed the entire scenario, you will have a picture of the overall shape and outcome in your head, created by intuition and the consultation. This picture not only is motivating and inspiring, it allows the cutting process to just move along.

Then, and only then, are you ready to pick up the shears.

The client also feels ready. You've asked the right questions and listened carefully to the answers. With **intuition and vision aligned**, you will be able to spend the rest of the time sculpting and making your creation work.

Both you and your client are ready to begin the transformation process. The process will now just unfold.

6. Consider taking "Before" and "After" pictures.

> *"My goal is to show the clear transformation to the client."*

During the consultation and before you begin sculpting, you may want to ask the client's permission to take a picture and then another picture after you are finished. I take a picture of the left side, right side, and back, and never include faces for privacy reasons.

While you might want to use these photos on social media for advertising, I don't use them only for this reason. The client can see how fresh their shape looks after just a dry cut, with no blow drying and styling. They can see and say, "Wow, this is something I will be able to do myself!"

Photos also allow you to show your client all the problem areas you have addressed. And the best part: when you, the artist, see the "after" pictures, you can look at the cut from all angles. You can see easily if there is any last-minute tweaking you need to do.

7. Always ask the client's permission to begin cutting.

> "Before I start sculpting, I need to check with my client to make sure he or she is comfortable with everything we discussed regarding his or her new look."

You are prepared. Now it's time to get reassurance from the client that he or she also is ready. It's important to ask your client at this point if they are comfortable and confident with what you both discussed, and that they do not have any questions or apprehensions. Now, and only now, can you begin your artistry.

8. As you begin to cut, trust your senses, especially your intuition.

> "My intuition is on. My shears are leading the way. They express every thought and whim I have. I am designing, creating, and letting my shears guide me. The shaping process begins and continues to unfold. My artistic and aesthetic intuition takes control. My hands and shears are an extension of my inner guided wisdom. My intuition helps guide my shears with every snip, notch, layer, texture,

> *and wisp added. I feel the hair to detect weight or varied texture. It allows me to easily create flow, movement, and lift."*

You may have heard of the fairly new trend known as "Intuitive Cutting" – the concept that hair should be cut according to growth patterns. Dry cutting often is referred to as "Intuitive Cutting" for a very good reason. As you've been learning, dry cutting is a powerful technique in which the hair is cut according to what it is doing naturally. "Intuitive Cutting" not only describes the way in which I cut the hair dry, but it also refers to my inner intuition, which carries me through the entire process. Throughout this time, I am using my intuition, which you most likely do too. Listen to your instincts.

Now, let the client sit back and relax and feel the excitement!

You can say many things with shears that words cannot express.

> *"All my life, I have cut my own hair. Everyone (clients and other hairdressers) asks me: 'How do you do it? How do you see the back? How do you know what you are doing?' My answer is that I cut my hair by feel and with my 'internal GPS'. I sense the hair and know (without even seeing the back) where it needs my attention. I don't think. I don't*

obsess. I let my shears respond to my intuitive navigation. It just happens effortlessly."

With this process, you can *feel* the weight, the length, the bulk, the lift or lack of lift, where texture is needed, if the hair is even or uneven, if it is symmetrical or asymmetrical (depending on the desired look), and the hair responding to each snip.

Once you get the hang of it, "Intuitive Cutting" is similar to tying your shoes or brushing your teeth blindfolded. These are things most of us can do without looking, based on our sense of touch because they just come naturally to us.

Cutting down the middle is a good way to start the cut and should minimize any random pieces when you do the final checking. Of course, there are exceptions. For example, if you are doing an asymmetrical cut, there will be intentionally longer pieces in the design. If this is the look the client wants, do not worry about stray pieces.

Touching and feeling the composition of the hair can help us when cutting. Of course, watching the hair move is equally as important, but other senses also can help when creating.

The many benefits of The Jen-uine Dry Cut™

9. Only one client at a time.

> *"My client is the only one in my chair. No exceptions. My time is dedicated 100% to that one cut. No interruptions. No head to wash. No color to put on."*

Many clients do not like to wait or to have more than one stylist work on them. At busy salons, many clients get frustrated when they are left waiting to process or left waiting for the next person to work on them. They want to feel as though their time is valuable. The same is true for stylists. We don't like it when clients are late. Should you ever find yourself running behind schedule, always call your next client. Maybe the new client's hair wasn't dry when he came in, or she had way more hair than she'd indicated over the phone. These things happen.

Clients will appreciate you letting them know that you are running 15 minutes behind. They might be running behind too, and could use the extra time instead of sitting in your waiting area.

It's not uncommon to encounter complications when working on multiple clients simultaneously. A perfect example of a disaster waiting to happen is when you work on someone's hair, while someone else is sitting under the dryer and processing under heat. You already know what will happen when lightener is left on the hair too long. Once the over-processed hair has been damaged, it's too late to fix the problem. It's an absolutely awful feeling for both you and your client and, of course, is completely avoidable.

Each individual who sits in our chair has a different "vibe" and personality. It can be confusing to work with multiple people with various energies. Creating an environment where it is just you and your client allows you to pick up on just his or her vibe. Your client will be more relaxed, too, if not exposed to others' energy or possible negativity.

And it is much easier to communicate and get to the heart of what your client desires. With just the two of you, you can make sure that the client is completely happy before he or she leaves: a challenge if you are working on multiple clients or if someone else is doing the blow drying and finishing work.

As the stylist who created your client's new look, you should be the one checking them out. This gives you the opportunity to observe and listen to their positive reaction to their new look. You're also able to talk to them about your plan for the next appointment. This shows you care and creates loyalty.

Clients deserve a thorough, lasting cut which is both easy to care for and which will have **movement and shape for months to come**. So, each needs and deserves your full attention.

10. Less anxiety for clients (and for you!).

> *"A rushed job is never a good job. I take all the time I need, so that I feel calm, and therefore, so does my client."*

Good news for the nervous and/or anxious client (and we all have them). With a dry cut, **what you see is what you get**. Your client can watch his or her new look unfold as you sculpt. There are no unforeseen surprises.

When hair is cut wet, clients have no idea what is happening, and how it is going to look until the appointment and cut time are already over. The hair might be much shorter when dry or not as layered as they had wished. Unfortunately, they might not speak up right away, and figure they will have to wait until next time. We do not want to wait for a next time; we want satisfaction and smiles now.

Regarding your own possible anxiety: should you ever feel unsure about something during the cutting process, pause and check in with the client for clarification. This should rarely, if ever, happen if you've done a thorough consultation. Since uncertainty can interrupt the artistic flow, this clarification is crucial to getting back to the flow of the cut. The certainty that comes with a dry cut is worth a lot to clients – and to you!

11. THE JEN-UINE DRY CUT™ calls for no products.

> "Since I began in this field, I've never been interested in "pushing" products, and I was not interested in competing with my fellow stylists as to who could sell the most products for the day. That said, I'm not against products. It's just that I believe that a thorough haircut should look good with little or no product."

With **THE JEN-UINE DRY CUT™**, the hair cooperates and does what it should do on its own.

Obviously, if a client wants advice on products or you feel like a certain product will help the integrity of their hair, you should always make recommendations. Sometimes, clients will ask for suggestions on good shampoos for colored hair or what product to use for their curls. You can always stock up on favorite products so that they're available if a client wants to purchase them at their appointment. When clients recognize you are not trying to make money by pushing a certain line or product on them, they feel more at ease because they will get a genuine professional opinion.

12. The JEN-UINE DRY CUT™ calls for no hair wash.

> *"I prefer to spend my time shaping and sculpting rather than washing and blow drying, which does not use my skill, but takes up a lot of time and energy. My firm belief is that the client should be paying me for my expertise and what I excel in, not something any other hairdresser can do."*

If a client is coming just for the head massage and wash, maybe **THE JEN-UINE DRY CUT™** is not for them. Some clients might not want to sit as long as it takes to dry cut their hair. And that is okay. We are all different, and we all are drawn to different approaches.

However, if a client really wants a hair wash, you certainly can offer it, but always for an extra fee. Why? It takes more of your time. You can wash and run the dryer through their hair with your fingers and then cut it. Or, if the client prefers, you can wash the hair after you've done the dry cut, also for an additional fee.

If a client wants a wash, head massage, and style, you can suggest that he or she book a separate appointment. Some love the hair wash! There is nothing better than a good scalp massage to release tension. However, your target clients are those who appreciate an in-depth cut and want an easy, lasting style.

13. The Jen-uine Dry Cut™ is organic – and portable.

"I love that **The Jen-uine Dry Cut™** *can be done anywhere!"*

The Jen-uine Dry Cut™ has integrity; it is **real and pure**. Since no products or water are needed, all you need are your shears and your canvas.

Some dry cutters do not work this way. They might choose to wash the hair before or after the cut, and therefore, need a wash sink. Other stylists might use products as well.

The Jen-uine Dry Cut™ can be done anywhere: in a salon, on the beach, at the park, in someone's backyard, or in someone's kitchen. This flexibility allows you to travel to clients. Clients *love* this opportunity, especially those who cannot leave their home.

14. The Jen-uine Dry Cut™ is a CUSTOM CUT, which no one else can replicate!

"One of the main reasons I've maintained a large clientele is that my cuts are different, and customized to each canvas."

The Jen-uine Dry Cut™ can be compared to a bespoke suit or dress. Getting measured allows one to get a custom fit, based on his or her body size and shape. This produces the most comfortable and appealing wear.

Similarly, each **haircut is tailored to the client's face shape and hair type** for the most flattering and effective results. As we know, everyone's hair lays differently, so snips are based on the way the hair falls naturally.

Here's the best part: **Your dry cut cannot be duplicated by anyone else**. You, too, can create an authentic haircut specific to each client's head shape, hair texture, and color placement. Simply put, THE JEN-UINE DRY CUT™ is not calculated, and there is no specific formula. It is tailored to the one client in your chair, and no two cuts are the same.

Consider that the right and left sides of our heads are not the same. Maybe the right side is curlier or the left side has a cowlick.

A systematic way of cutting does not take these variants into consideration.

How can you possibly cut everyone's hair the same way when every section and every strand is different and has its own identity? As you shape, you can watch how the hair moves. You can study the hair and react based on how each snip you make is responding to the hair. No two people are the same, and no two canvases of hair are the same.

Here is one of the main reasons you can be confident in raising your prices. Who won't pay more for something created **just for them**?

Celebrate Your Artistry

15. Quality vs Quantity.

> *"With **The Jen-uine Dry Cut**™, I roll out the red carpet for each and every client. I try to make everyone in my chair feel special."*

- Each and every client who sits in your chair deserves and should get the best version of you and your craft. Simply put, give yourself enough time with each customer. No one likes to be rushed. You need enough time to do your job correctly. Consider:

- How can art be timed?
- How can every client take the same amount of time when everyone's hair is different?
- How can you possibly do a consultation in five minutes and a cut in 15-30 minutes?

Thinking about these questions, it is obvious that clients appreciate it when you take your time. They feel taken care of and special. They appreciate this approach, knowing that you are not just rushing to get to your next client.

You might be hesitant to try this approach, because you wonder how you can earn enough money if you spend so much time with one client. It has been my experience that your clients will pay more for the attentiveness to detail and for your time.

Clients are paying you for your training and expertise. This is what sets us apart as artists. They will spend the extra money for your **undivided attention and for your sincere care** that they are happy.

16. A Delicate Touch.

> "I once offered to be a hair model for a stylist I was training. While I have a "hard head," I could feel that she was combing way too roughly. She might have been nervous or was not conscious of how hard she was pulling. I kindly pointed it out to her, and she ended up thanking me. She expressed to me later that she had developed more awareness. Moving forward, she worked with caution and softness. In return, a few of her clients commented on her gentleness when working with their hair."

A haircut should not hurt, and should be nothing but relaxing for our clients. Always maintain a delicate touch when combing, touching, and shaping someone's hair. Some clients have a very sensitive scalp, and so keep this in mind when handling their hair. Also, you must work with caution if you have longer nails. You may not realize that your nails might accidentally scratch or hurt clients.

This might seem obvious, but the truth is too many stylists are unaware of how combing roughly or approaching a tangle without care might not end well. We must have extreme patience when handling our clients' hair so that we do not pull too hard and unintentionally harm them.

Always maintaining a soft touch will avoid any disruptions to the relaxed, "zen" feeling we aim to provide.

17. Creating Cascading Layers.

> *"Cascading layers can work for any length, structure, or type of hair, and I find that using* **THE JEN-UINE DRY CUT**™ *makes styling and care so much easier."*

You probably remember this term from cosmetology school. Cascading layers are layers that are added throughout the mid-lengths and ends of the hair, so that the hair "intertwines". These intertwining layers are ideal for anyone who wants to keep their length, but also wants to gain volume and movement. Cascading (or blended) layers are also the best solution for blending extensions with the client's natural hair.

When the hair makes transitions without any bulk, it can breathe. It can move, lift, and express itself. It will not just clump together and lay there.

Cascading layers will eliminate steps or demarcation lines that cannot be seen when the hair is wet. They will create a certain softness to your layers. This is an important factor in almost every **Jen-uine Dry Cut**™.

Finishing:
The Cut's Final Stages – and Beyond

18. Checking the hair.

> *"How do I know when my work is done? I not only can see it; I can feel it!"*

For all hair types, be sure not to base your cut just on one specific part line. Even if the client says that he or she parts it only one way, you must check. Sure, some people part their hair more to the left or more to the right, but is it always going to be parted in that exact place? It's unlikely.

If someone is in the wind, dancing, at the ocean, had a restless night's sleep or simply is flipping their hair back and forth, there should be no stray long pieces that do not go with the shape. Your client's hair should look good *all the time*.

Direct the hair to the left, redirect to the right, and then direct the hair straight back to look for any fragments which might be out of place. This is the first part of the checking process.

It also helps to step back from your canvas and take a look at the overall shape. Is it characteristic of your vision? Where in your creation do you focus? Looking at the whole canvas at a distance is an important aspect at this time.

You will know your cut is complete when you are able to put down the shears and do not feel the need to pick them up again. You will have created a new structure, magically weightless. You will have confidence knowing your client will love his or her hair.

19. The Reveal.

> *"Quite frequently, I will ask my clients if they want to be surprised. The answer is almost always 'yes'. Since I always make sure there is mutual trust during the consultation, most clients are excited to be captivated. My clients love the idea of getting a makeover and new look."*

Ask your clients whether they want to see the progress during the intuitive cutting stage, and they might choose to take a peek. Oftentimes, as you are sculpting away from the mirror, you might choose to wait until the end to show them their new look.

Your shears are down now because you are satisfied that you have addressed all areas thoroughly. It is now time to reveal the new look to your client.

This is the best part! It is so rewarding to watch the clients' reactions when they look in the mirror.

We want to help our clients to see the beauty that everyone else sees. This is what the **right cut can do for anyone**.

20. Make sure every client is completely happy and your work is consistent every time.

> *"From the beginning of my career, my motto has been to not let my clients leave unless they are 100% happy."*

You want your client to leave feeling awesome. Isn't this the best feeling, when you know that you've "nailed it"? Your client is happy. He or she just exudes so much more confidence than when they walked in.

This is absolutely the number one reason why we love what we do. We just want to make others feel better about themselves. Wouldn't it be great to have everyone who leaves your chair feel this way ... every time?

Consistency is so important. Avoid giving your clients exceptional service the first time they come in, and then cutting corners for their next appointments. They are coming back to you because you make them feel good and you provide consistent work. They will notice the difference if this changes.

And always be sure to book the next appointment before the client pays. When you discuss their "hair plan," and what you'll be doing next time, they will be excited to return.

21. Follow up the next day.

"Even though I am confident that my guest loves his or her new look (or else I would not have let them leave my chair), I still always follow up with new clients the next day."

This is *so* important. This reminds your new client just how much you really do care. While they felt cared for in your chair, when you call (or email) the next day, it shows them that you're still thinking about them. This simple gesture **reinforces your commitment** to make your client feel special.

You want to make absolutely sure that they are in love with their hair. If they feel as though they want to go a little shorter or have a few more face-framing layers, you want to know so you can invite them back in to see you, free of charge. This element of **THE JEN-UINE DRY CUT**™ shows your clients how committed you are to them.

Positive feedback is empowering, and helps to fuel you. Hearing the happiness and appreciation in your client's voice the next day, reinforces your craft and shows you that this method works.

22. Make your clients feel special.

"My practice is to send my clients a card on their birthday, a thank you card for a referral, and sometimes, even a note for leaving me a generous tip!"

When you make your clients feel special, you will become a big part of their life. Taking five minutes out of your day to send a card or greeting goes a long way. Reward your clients for being a loyal customer. You can do this by offering 20% off for referring a friend, or offering 50% off after six visits. These simple gestures **reinforce your relationship**. Clients return to you because of an emotion attached to their experience with you. The way you show appreciation to your clients is limited only by your imagination! Your clients will talk to others. They will love being rewarded for sending you business.

23. Treat your clients as customers, not as income.

*"For more than twenty years, I've created a clientele of **JEN-UINE** believers."*

A client who feels pressured into buying more products or more services is a client who will not return. Following **THE JEN-UINE DRY CUT™** method, your clients will come back, and they will pay your higher rates because they see and appreciate what you do for them. They will trust you to do anything that they want done with their hair. They may approach you about coloring their hair or maybe getting a keratin treatment. When you show them that you care about them and their specific needs, you've established trust from the very beginning.

24. Privacy really, really matters.

> *"So many times, I've witnessed hairdressers sharing with others things they should not have said. If your client feels betrayed, they definitely will not be back."*

Clients *love* talking to their hairdressers. Sometimes, they open up to us about things they've not shared with anyone. Clients often refer their friends and family to us. We owe it to them to never disclose things that they have discussed with us. This seems obvious, but please be careful to not share your client's private information with anyone.

25. Ensure that your clients want to return for years to come.

> *"Throughout the entire process from meeting to revealing, I am using my intuition. You most likely do too. Listen to it – it can truly help you."*

Clients today have many choices as to where to get their hair done. Using this special and different approach will set you apart from other stylists.

When your clients sense your **genuine intention** to make a positive difference, they will be back. This is your gift to them, and their delighted smile is their gift to you. As you show compassion for everyone in your chair, you will build a flourishing clientele.

How you treat your clients reflects who you are. Your clientele will help you grow as an artist and as a person. Learning new techniques such as dry cutting shows just how passionate you are about what you do. Part of expanding your clientele is showing your clients that you are an expert in the industry. Clients look to us not only for our artistic skills and knowledge, but also for support in their personal lives. You are creating a cherished, even sacred relationship.

Conclusion

Did anything in this book speak to you?

I truly hope that my words have fueled your inner creative passion. If you feel something stirring inside you, go and use your intuition and artistic abilities to create! Perhaps some of my ideas, which have worked so well for me, have awakened your imagination and have piqued some originality in you as a stylist.

My wish is that you will find **THE JEN-UINE DRY CUT**™ helpful for you. You do not have to follow all of these recommendations; you can choose the specific elements that work for you.

You now have the choice to try this approach with certain clients, and see how it flows. My guess is that you will enjoy your craft even more because you are making everyone in your chair happy. You will feel energized when you watch your client retention rate double, and your schedule fills quickly.

Please remember to compete only with yourself to **be the best version of you** that you can possibly be. Contending with others will interrupt the process of finding your true passion and the methods which work the best for you.

We are all artists, and I encourage you to try new approaches to doing your craft. You don't need to work in the way you were taught in school. You will know when you're doing the best work you can. Art has no "right" or "wrong". You have a chance to create and use your own unique abilities. Open yourself up to the possibility that you can be surprised at what's inside you, and what you can share with your clients.

You can create customized cuts as original as each person you meet. Intuition does not lie. If you feel it, go for it!

Jen Brumm Lancia
Creator of **THE JEN-UINE DRY CUT**™

www.ingramcontent.com/pod-product-compliance
Lightning Source LLC
Chambersburg PA
CBHW020456220526
45464CB00002B/1007